Monuments of Washington, D.C.

Use Place Value Understanding and Properties of Operations to Add and Subtract

Devon McKinney

NEW YORK

Published in 2015 by The Rosen Publishing Group, Inc.
29 East 21st Street, New York, NY 10010

Book Design: Mickey Harmon

Photo Credits: Cover, pp. 5, 9, 11, 13, 15, 17, 21 (Capitol Building) Orhan Cam/Shutterstock.com; p. 7 Mesut Dogan/
Shutterstock.com; p. 19 Steve Heap/Shutterstock.com; p. 21 (White House) kropic1/Shutterstock.com; p. 21 (Washington
Monument) Steve Collender/Shutterstock.com; p. 22 spirit of america/Shutterstock.com.

Library of Congress Cataloging-in-Publication Data

McKinney, Devon, author.
 Monuments of Washington, D.C. : use place value understanding and properties of operations to add and subtract /
Devon McKinney.
     pages cm. — (Math masters, number and operations in base ten)
 Includes index.

ISBN 978-1-4777-4771-1 (pbk.)
ISBN 978-1-4777-4774-2 (6-pack)
ISBN 978-1-4777-6435-0 (library binding)

1. Mathematics—Juvenile literature. 2. Place value (Mathematics)—Juvenile literature. 3. Washington (D.C.)—Buildings,
structures, etc.—Juvenile literature. I. Title.
 QA40.5.M43 2015
 513.2—dc23
                                    2013041762

Manufactured in the United States of America

CPSIA Compliance Information: Batch #WS15RC: For further information contact Rosen Publishing, New York, New York at 1-800-237-9932.

Contents

The Capital City

Do you know what the capital of the United States is? It's Washington, D.C. That's where the U.S. government makes rules and laws for our country.

Washington, D.C., is home to some of our country's most important buildings. Many places are old, and some of them are monuments. A monument is a **statue**, building, or other **structure** that was made to honor a famous person or event.

There are monuments all over the United States, but many of them are in Washington, D.C.

Some monuments in Washington, D.C., are very big. Many have a lot of windows, floors, **columns**, and other cool **features**. Because these buildings are so large, the number of features they have is large, too. Adding and subtracting these features is a fun way to learn interesting facts about our capital's important monuments. You can use place value to help you add and subtract.

Numbers are made of **digits**. Each digit stands for a group, and the groups are known as place values. The number 1,234 has a ones place, a tens place, a hundreds place, and a thousands place.

thousands hundreds tens ones

1,234

The White House

The White House is where the president of the United States lives and works. The White House has 412 doors and 147 windows. How many features is that altogether? Add the ones place first. Adding 2 plus 7 makes 9. Next, add the tens. Adding 1 plus 4 makes 5. Finally, add the hundreds. Adding 4 plus 1 makes 5. That means the White House has 559 doors and windows.

$$\begin{array}{r} 412 \\ +\ 147 \\ \hline 559 \end{array}$$

We always read numbers from left to right, but we add and subtract from right to left, starting with the ones place.

We know that the White House has 559 doors and windows because we added 147 to 412. There's another way to make 559, though. We can get the same answer by adding 412 to 147. Before, we added 2 plus 7 to make 9. In this equation, we add 7 plus 2. That still makes 9. Can you do the same in the tens and hundreds places?

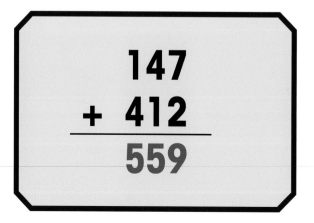

$$\begin{array}{r} 147 \\ + \ 412 \\ \hline 559 \end{array}$$

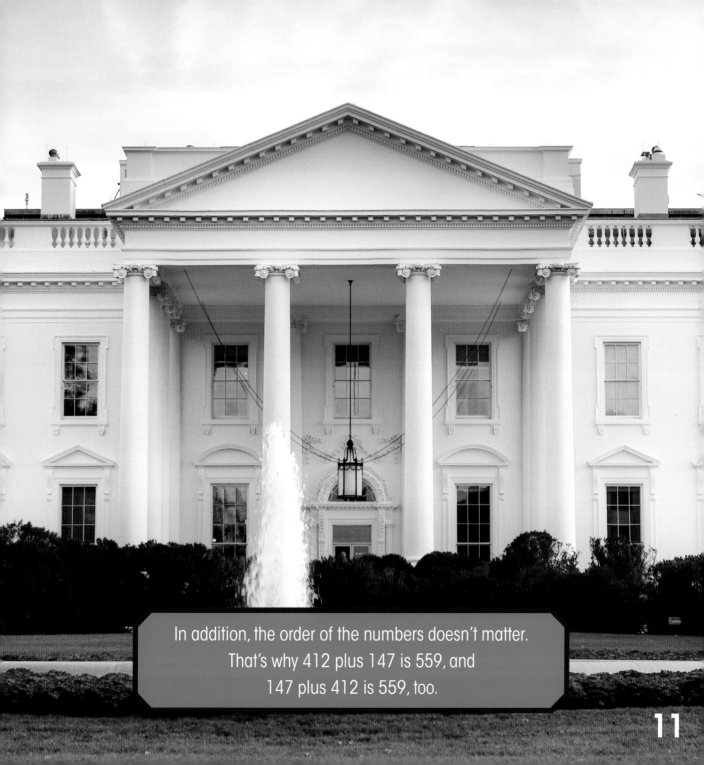

In addition, the order of the numbers doesn't matter.
That's why 412 plus 147 is 559, and
147 plus 412 is 559, too.

Monuments with Columns

Some monuments have columns. The Jefferson Memorial honors President Thomas Jefferson. It has a **portico** with 12 columns. It has 26 columns along the back of it. Adding 12 and 26 makes 38.

The Lincoln Memorial, which honors President Abraham Lincoln, also has columns. It has 36. Adding 38 and 36 makes 74. How did we get that answer?

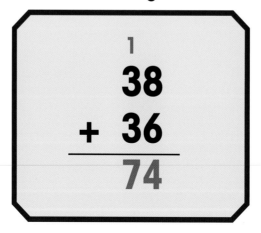

Jefferson Memorial

Adding 8 and 6 makes 14 ones, but the ones place only has room for 1 number. You must carry the 1 to the tens place, where you add 1 and 3 and 3. That's how you make 7 tens and 4 ones, or 74 columns total.

You can use subtraction to check your addition from the last problem. We know the Jefferson Memorial and the Lincoln Memorial have 74 columns altogether. We also know the Jefferson Memorial has 38 columns. You can subtract the Jefferson Memorial's columns from the total number of columns to find out what's left. It should match the number you used in your addition equation.

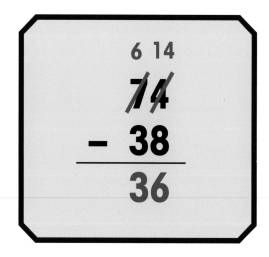

Lincoln Memorial

Since 4 ones is less than 8 ones, you must borrow a ten from the tens place. Adding a ten to 4 makes 14, and 14 minus 8 is 6. That leaves a 6 in the tens place, and 6 minus 3 is 3. That's how we make 36.

Hundreds of Steps

Some monuments are so big that they have hundreds of steps. Steps take us up and down a monument's many floors. The Washington Monument is a very tall building in Washington, D.C. It has 897 stairs!

Another building with a lot of stairs is the U.S. Capitol, which is where Congress works. It has 365 stairs. Can you use place value to add these numbers?

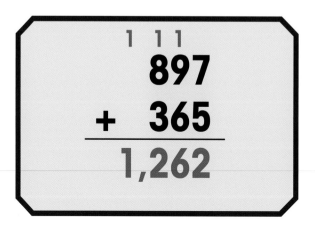

$$\begin{array}{r} \overset{1}{}\overset{1}{}\overset{1}{} \\ 897 \\ +\ 365 \\ \hline 1{,}262 \end{array}$$

U.S. Capitol

Adding 7 and 5 in the ones place makes 12. Carry the 1 to the tens place. It may seem hard to add 3 numbers here, but if you add 9 and 1 first to make 10, then you only have 2 numbers to add. Can you finish this equation on your own?

The Washington Monument has more steps than the U.S. Capitol. We know this because the hundreds place shows that 897 is greater than 365.

You can use subtraction to find out how many more steps the Washington Monument has. First, 7 ones minus 5 ones is 2. Next, 9 tens minus 6 tens is 3. Finally, 8 hundreds minus 3 hundreds is 5. What is the answer?

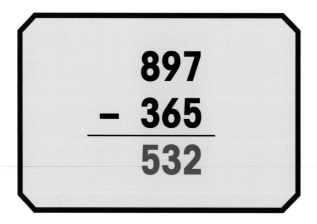

$$\begin{array}{r} 897 \\ -\ 365 \\ \hline 532 \end{array}$$

Washington Monument

The Washington Monument has 532 more steps than the U.S. Capitol.
Using place value and subtraction helped us find the answer.

Lots of Floors

Many of the monuments in Washington, D.C., have more than 1 floor. The Capitol has 5 floors, the White House has 4 floors, and the Washington Monument has 3 floors. How many floors is that altogether? You can add 5 floors and 4 floors to make 9. Then, add the 3 remaining floors to make 12.

$$(5 + 4) + 3 = 12$$
$$5 + (4 + 3) = 12$$

Washington Monument

U.S. Capitol

White House

There's another way to do this math. You can start by adding 4 floors and 3 floors to make 7. Then, add the remaining 5 floors. You still get 12—the same answer!

Monumental Math

The United States has many monuments, but some of the most interesting are in Washington, D.C. Many are old and can teach us a lot about history. The city and its monuments are a great way to learn about our country's past. They're also a great way to practice math! They have many features that make addition and subtraction fun.

Glossary

column (KAH-luhm) A tall, round post that holds up a roof.

digit (DIH-juht) Any number from 0 to 9.

feature (FEE-chur) A part of somehing.

portico (POHR-tih-koh) A covered walkway or porch
with columns.

statue (STAA-choo) A figure made of stone, wood, or other
matter that represents a person or animal.

structure (STRUHK-chur) A building or monument.

Index

Due to the changing nature of Internet links, The Rosen Publishing Group, Inc., has developed an online list of websites related to the subject of this book. This site is updated regularly. Please use this link to access the list: **www.powerkidslinks.com/mm/nobt/monu**